OLYMPIC SPORTS

GYMNASTICS

by Clive Gifford

amicus

Published by Amicus
P.O. Box 1329
Mankato, MN 56002

Printed in the United States of America at Corporate Graphics, in North Mankato, Minnesota.

Library of Congress Cataloging-in-Publication Data
Gifford, Clive.
 Gymnastics / by Clive Gifford.
    p. cm. -- (Olympic sports)
 Includes index.
 Summary: "An introduction to women's and men's gymnastics events held at the summer Olympics, including the floor exercise, vault, balance beam, parallel bars, and more. Also explains rules, records, and famous Olympic gymnasts" --Provided by publisher.
 ISBN 978-1-60753-191-3 (library binding)
 1. Gymnastics--Juvenile literature. 2. Olympics--Juvenile literature. I. Title.
 GV461.3.G54 2012
 796.41--dc22

                                                        2011000590

Created by Appleseed Editions, Ltd.
Designed by Helen James
Edited by Mary-Jane Wilkins
Picture research by Su Alexander

Picture credits
page 4 AFP/Getty Images; 5 Valeria73/Shutterstock; 6 AFP/Getty Images; 7 John Lamb/ Getty Images; 8 Getty Images; 9 AFP/Getty Images; 10 Getty Images; 11l Getty Images, r Jiang Dao Hua/Shutterstock; 12 AFP/Getty Images; 13 Jiang Dao Hua/Shutterstock; 14 AFP/Getty Images; 15t Bloomberg via Getty Images, b Alexander Ishchenko/ Shutterstock; 16 & 17 AFP/Getty Images; 18 Getty Images; 19 AFP/Getty Images; 20 Getty Images; 21 AFP/Getty Images; 22 Getty Images; 23t De Visu/Shutterstock, b Getty Images; 24 & 25 Getty Images; 26 Bloomberg via Getty Images; 27 Sports Illustrated/Getty Images; 28 Getty Images; 29t Getty Images, b AFP/Getty Images:
Front cover: AFP/Getty Images

DAD0051
3-2011

9 8 7 6 5 4 3 2 1

Contents

Going for Gold

The Olympics is the greatest sporting event on Earth. Thousands of competitors, called Olympians, flock to one city every four years to compete over 17 days of unforgettable action. The very best athletes win an Olympic gold, silver, or bronze medal.

China's Li Xiaopeng flies high above the parallel bars during the 2008 Olympics. Xiaopeng won this artistic gymnastics event, and Yoo Wonchul from South Korea came second.

thousands of spectators, while hundreds of millions more watch on television.

MODERN GAMES

The modern Olympic Games began in 1896 in Athens. They revived the sports contests held by the ancient Greeks at Olympia from 776 BC. Today, the summer Olympics are held every four years. The host city and nation welcome

SKILL AND STRENGTH

Gymnastics has been a part of every modern Olympics for men, and since 1928 for women. Gymnasts perform great feats of strength, balance, **flexibility**, and poise. They need high

levels of **coordination** in their movements and explosive power for some leaping events, such as vaulting. At the 2012 Olympics, a total of 324 gymnasts will compete in the different medal competitions.

THREE TYPES

There are three different types of gymnastic events held at an Olympics: **artistic gymnastics**, **rhythmic gymnastics**, and trampolining. Rhythmic gymnasts make graceful, flowing moves to music. They perform on a large mat using objects such as a ball and large hoop. In artistic gymnastics, competitors often perform spectacular routines or moves on equipment called **apparatus**. Trampolining gymnasts bounce high above a trampoline where they twist and turn in somersaults.

GAMES AGE

In the past, medal-winning Olympic gymnasts have ranged in age from ten to over thirty. In 1997, the International Gymnastics Federation (**FIG**), the organization that runs world gymnastics, decided that gymnasts must be 16 years or older to compete in major championships, including the Olympics.

Olympic OoPs

Dong Fangxiao was a bronze medalist at the 2000 Olympics with the Chinese team. When she became an official at the 2008 Olympics, an investigation found that she was only 14 years old in 2000, two years below the minimum age. She and the rest of her team lost their medals.

Simeonova Seredova performs with the hoop during a rhythmic gymnastics competition in Italy in 2009. Rhythmic gymnasts must keep the hoop moving as they perform.

Superstar

No one has won more Olympic medals in any sport than Russian gymnast Larisa Latynina. She competed at the games in 1956, 1960, and 1964 and won an incredible nine gold, five silver, and four bronze medals.

Artistic Gymnastics

Artistic gymnastics are the most popular and well-known gymnastics events at the Olympics. Gymnasts perform on different pieces of equipment, and their routines are scored by a panel of judges.

The judges watch carefully as Jiang Yuyuan of China performs a somersault during her vault. She came in third in this 2007 World Cup competition, with a score of 14.412.

Different Events

At the Olympics, male gymnasts compete on six different pieces of apparatus and women on four. Both men and women perform floor exercises and vaults on the vaulting table. Women also perform on the uneven bars and the balance beam. Only men compete on the parallel bars, high bar, pommel horse, and rings.

Reaching the Final

Gymnasts arrive at an Olympics knowing that they must perform incredibly well in the first competition, called the preliminary. Only the eight highest-scoring gymnasts in this enter the final on each piece of apparatus. Scores from the preliminaries don't count in the final. Gymnasts start all over again, with the highest score winning gold. In the 2008 men's floor competition, Chinese gymnast Zou Kai qualified in sixth place and the Brazilian Diego Hypólito in first, yet in the final, Kai took the gold medal and Hypólito ended sixth.

SCORING SYSTEMS

A gymnast's score used to be marked out of ten. This was changed after the 2004 Olympics. Now, the scores are a total of two marks. The first reflects the difficulty and technical demands of the gymnast's routine. The second score, called the **execution** or B score, is based on how well the gymnast performs the routine. A panel of six judges marks the execution score out of 10.00, taking marks off for mistakes or falls.

Elite gymnasts usually score more than 15.5 points. At the 2008 Olympics, Shawn Johnson of the United States scored 16.225 to win the balance beam gold medal.

A gymnast makes a perfect dismount from the uneven bars. Her feet are together and her back is arched, with her head up and arms and hands stretched out. A good dismount helps artistic gymnasts gain higher scores.

Floor Exercises

Rebecca Bross performs a split leap with her legs parallel to the floor during her routine at the 2010 U.S. National Championships. The sixteen-year-old went on to win a silver medal in the competition.

The floor exercise (or FX for short) became an individual event for men in 1936 and in 1952 for women. Gymnasts perform on a 12 meter (39.37 ft.) square mat placed on a sprung floor. This helps to cushion landings after gymnasts have made spectacular leaps, flips, and somersaults or **saltos**.

FEATS AND RECORDS

Gymnasts from Romania have won the women's floor gold medal six times since the 1980 Olympics. The latest winner was Sandra Izbaşa who narrowly beat U.S. gymnasts Shawn Johnson and Nastia Liukin at the 2008 games.

WOMEN'S ROUTINES

The women's floor routine lasts up to 90 seconds and is set to music. Gymnasts must perform a series of movements that match the music perfectly, as well as show off their personality and display artistic skill, great balance, strength, and flexibility.

MEN'S ROUTINES

The men's floor routine usually lasts between 60 and 70 seconds, but it is not set to music. Although there are some graceful elements, it is more a test of strength, with held handstands and controlled balance positions, as well as spectacular tumbling.

TERRIFIC TUMBLING

The judges mark gymnasts on their artistic flair, and on how well they hold positions and flow between movements. The spectators are most thrilled by the acrobatic **sequences** of jumps, twists, and somersaults that gymnasts perform. These are known as tumbling.

Tumbling sequences include moves such as **back flips** and the Rudi—a forward somersault with 1½ twists. Gymnasts build several major tumbling sequences into their routine, with the longest running diagonally across the mat from one corner to another.

HAPPY LANDINGS

At the end of each sequence of tumbling moves, gymnasts try to land without taking extra steps to keep their balance. Judges deduct marks for wobbly landings, for not using the entire mat, and for poorly performed moves.

Superstar

At the 1980 Olympics, two of the all-time greatest female gymnasts, Nellie Kim of Russia and Nadia Comaneci of Romania, both scored 19.875 out of a possible 20 marks in the floor competition. As a result, both were awarded gold medals.

Fabian Hambuechen performs his floor routine at the 2008 Olympics. The German gymnast was disappointed that his score of 15.650 put him in fourth place, just out of the medals.

The Vault

Leszek Blanik of Poland competes in the final of the men's vault on day ten of the 2008 Olympics. The approach to the vaulting table must be perfect since an error in timing or positioning can ruin the vault.

The vault is one of the most exciting and explosive of all gymnastics events. Gymnasts sprint down a long runway, jump onto a springboard, and push off a large vaulting table to perform a spectacular vault before landing.

HORSE TO TABLE

The vaulting horse developed from model horses designed to allow knights and soldiers on horseback to practice mounting and dismounting. Vaulting horses were replaced in competitions in 2001 by a larger, flatter vaulting table. The women's vaulting table is 49.21 inches (125 cm) high and the men's 53.15 inches (135 cm) high.

VAULT START

Gymnasts run along a 25 meter (82.02 ft.) runway, building speed and rhythm before they hit the springboard. They tell the judges what sort of vault they will perform and only begin when a signal is shown. At the 2008 Olympics, top Russian gymnast Anna Pavlova began her vault before the green light signal. The judges awarded her a score of zero.

PRE AND POST FLIGHT

The vault is divided into pre-flight (from the springboard to the table) and post-flight (after the gymnast has pushed off the table) sections. In the post-flight phase, the gymnast somersaults and twists in the air. The timing must be perfect so the vaulter lands upright on both feet without wobbling or taking extra steps.

Hong Un Jong lands well after her vault at the 2008 Olympics. She won gold in the women's vault, the first gold medal won by a North Korean female gymnast.

VAULTING FAMILIES

Vaults are divided into different families. In the Tsukahara family (named after Japanese five-time gold medalist Mitsuo Tsukahara), the gymnast performs half a twist between the springboard and the table so they face backward. In the Olympic final, gymnasts perform two vaults from different families.

High speed on the runway and a strong push-off from the vaulting table can send a gymnast soaring high into the air.

Superstar

In 1984, U.S. gymnast Mary Lou Retton went into the final round of the vault needing a high score to win the gold medal. She needed a perfect 10 score in her vault to win the all-around competition, a score she achieved with a flawless vault.

The Balance Beam

Female gymnasts often give their most dramatic performances on the balance beam. It is just 4 inches (10 cm) wide, yet the best gymnasts perform an incredible range of moves on it, including handsprings, flips, and somersaults.

A LONG TRADITION

The balance beam developed from German and Swedish low beams used for balancing exercises more than a century ago. It was introduced at the gymnastics world championships in 1934 and into the Olympics in 1952. At first, it was mainly used for simple but

Shawn Johnson launches herself upside down during her gold-medal-winning routine on the balance beam at the 2008 Olympics.

Superstar

Shawn Johnson won three silver medals at the 2008 Olympics and finally secured a gold medal in the balance beam competition. The governor of her home state of Iowa declared October 17 "Shawn Johnson Day" in celebration.

Many top gymnasts use a springboard to leap straight onto the beam. The first ever back flip onto a balance beam was performed by East Germany's Maxi Gnauck in 1981.

Beam Routines

Beam routines last up to 90 seconds. A clock is displayed where both the judges and the gymnast can see it, and a bell sounds after 80 seconds. Gymnasts perform a mixture of running and walking steps, leaps, jumps, and splits in the air. They must use the full length of the beam, showing off their flexibility, elegance, and in some cases, bravery.

Wobbles and Falls

Throughout a routine, the judges watch carefully, taking marks off for jerky movements or mistakes. One of the most common is a balance check, when a gymnast wobbles from side to side or forward and backward after a difficult move.

graceful dance-like movements. From the 1960s and after, more acrobatic moves were added by a new generation of bold gymnasts, such as Olga Korbut, Nadia Comaneci, and Nellie Kim.

Mounting the Beam

The beam is 16.4 feet (5 m) long and 3.9 feet (1.2 m) high. A gymnast begins a routine by mounting (getting onto) the beam without help.

This sequence of photos shows the extraordinary agility and shapes a gymnast can make on the balance beam as she travels its full length.

The Rings

The rings are the ultimate test of a male gymnast's strength. They are a pair of wooden or plastic circles about 9.4 inches (24 cm) in diameter. The gymnast grips the rings as he performs swinging movements and holds positions that require great strength.

Fabian Hambuechen of Germany performs a rings routine at the 2008 Olympics. He has locked his arms and is bringing his legs up and together for a hold position that requires immense strength.

Olympic OoPs

Shun Fujimoto broke his kneecap during the floor exercise at the 1976 Olympics. He did not want to let down the Japanese team, and despite being in agony, performed a superb routine on the rings, including a triple somersault dismount. His score of 9.7, his highest ever, won Japan the team gold.

HANGING DOWN

The rings hang on straps from an 18.86 ft. (5.75 m) tall tower. They hang 20 in. (50 cm) apart and 9.02 ft. (2.75 m) off the ground, so a coach lifts each gymnast to grip the rings at the start.

STRONG AND STILL

A rings routine is made up of a number of moves in which the gymnast holds as still a position as possible. This is incredibly difficult since the rings swing freely on their straps. Gymnasts need

Yang Wei has released the rings and is starting to perform a twist in the air as part of his dismount. The Chinese gymnast won a silver medal in the rings at the 2008 games.

great strength to keep movement to a minimum. Common strength positions are handstands above the rings and the iron cross. To do this, a gymnast holds the rings straight out on either side of his body while staying upright and still. A gymnast must hold a position for two seconds to receive points from the judges. To move between the different

Many gymnasts wear hand supports called ring guards and dust their hands with powder from a **chalk box** to provide extra grip when performing on the rings.

strength positions, gymnasts swing on the rings, but they also need perfect control when doing this to prevent the rings from swaying back and forth.

BIG FINISH

Stillness and perfect control in a range of holds are crucial parts of a winning routine, but gymnasts must also have a spectacular **dismount**. They build momentum by swinging around on the rings several times before launching themselves up and away. Many gymnasts perform a double or triple somersault with a twist before landing.

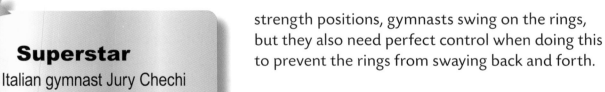

Superstar

Italian gymnast Jury Chechi became known as the "Lord of the Rings" during the 1990s when he competed in many rings events. He won five world championships and the 1996 Olympic gold medal.

The High and Uneven Bars

In two events, gymnasts swing around one or a pair of horizontal bars. The high bar is for men, and the uneven bars (also called the asymmetric bars) are for women.

THE HORIZONTAL HIGH BAR

The high bar is 7.9 ft. (2.4 m) long and 9.2 ft. (2.8 m) off the ground. A coach helps gymnasts up onto the bar where they perform a routine full of swinging movements and changes of grip. The most exciting moves on the high bar are the **releases**: a gymnast lets go of the bar, performs a spectacular move such as a somersault, and then grabs the bar again. Releases need split-second timing so the gymnast doesn't fall.

At the Olympics, each routine must include two high-risk release moves where the gymnast lets go of the bar. Gymnasts often combine this with a move such as a Gienger, in which they perform a back somersault with half a twist before grasping the bar again. Another common move is the pirouette. The gymnast performs a handstand, lets go with one hand and twists her body around to face the opposite direction.

CLOSE COMPETITION

Competition is often close on the high bar. At the 2008 Olympics, China's Zou Kai won a gold medal with a score of 16.200, while the U.S.' Jonathan Horton was close behind with 16.175.

THE UNEVEN BARS

Flexibility, strength, timing, and bravery are all needed to perform on the uneven bars, which stand 5.3 and 7.9 ft. (161 and 241 cm) high. A gymnast jumps to grasp the bar, then swings, bends, and leaps between the bars in an amazing routine. They flow from one move to the next and end with a high-flying dismount.

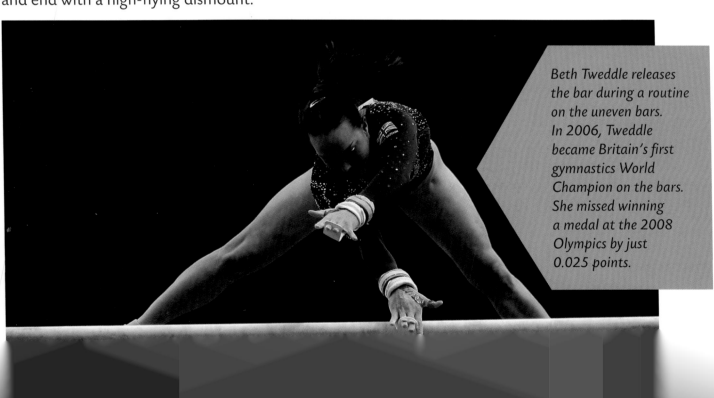

Beth Tweddle releases the bar during a routine on the uneven bars. In 2006, Tweddle became Britain's first gymnastics World Champion on the bars. She missed winning a medal at the 2008 Olympics by just 0.025 points.

Parallel Bars and Pommel Horse

Only male gymnasts compete on the pommel horse and parallel bars. Both require enormous arm and upper body strength to support the gymnast's body weight throughout a strenuous routine.

*Li Xiaopeng of China is in a **tucked** position as he performs an impressive dismount from the parallel bars. Xiaopeng won the 2008 Olympic gold medal in this event with a high score of 16.450.*

PARALLEL BARS

The parallel bars are two 11.5 foot (3.5 m) long bars that stand 6.4 feet (1.95 m) from the ground. The width between the two bars can be adjusted for each gymnast. A parallel bars routine includes a mixture of fast, spectacular movements such as swings, rolls, and somersaults and slower strength moves, such as holding a controlled handstand position.

HIGH AND LOW

Gymnasts work both above and below the bars, being careful not to touch the ground with their feet since this will lose them points. They can take their hands off the bars to twist their bodies and change the direction they face, as well as launch themselves high above the bars to perform a somersault. They end their routine by building momentum with swings so that they can perform a spectacular dismount, which often involves a double somersault.

THE POMMEL HORSE

The pommel horse is 5.25 ft. (160 cm) long, 3.7 ft. (115 cm) tall, and has two pommels, or handles, in its center. The gymnast grips these during the routine. At times, the gymnast moves away from the center and places his hands on the main part of the horse. The rules say that they must use the entire length of the horse during a routine.

SHORT AND SMOOTH ROUTINES

Pommel horse routines seem short at around 25 seconds, but a gymnast needs great strength to support his whole body weight with just his arms. Gymnasts make series of circular and swinging movements with their legs sometimes together with toes pointed. At other times, their legs are apart; this is known as a flair. Moves flow smoothly into one another. Judges **penalize** jerky movements or poor hand positions.

All-Around Events

The ultimate achievement for individual gymnasts is the all-around competition at the Olympics. This tests their abilities on all the different apparatus. A similar competition for national teams is just as highly valued.

Deng Linlin (right) clenches her fists with delight as her Chinese team wins the team gold medal at the Beijing Olympics. Deng performed on the vault, floor, and balance beam in the competition.

THE INDIVIDUAL COMPETITION

The 24 top-scoring gymnasts from the preliminary competition enter the all-around final, with one exception. Each country is only allowed two gymnasts in the top 24. At the 2004 women's all-around event, four U.S. gymnasts finished first, fourth, eighth, and thirteenth in the preliminaries, but only the top two, Carly Patterson and Courtney Kupets, could compete in the final.

ULTIMATE CHAMPION

In the final, each gymnast competes on every piece of apparatus, with each score contributing to his or her overall total. All gymnasts have stronger and weaker events. In the 2008 women's all-around competition, the winner, Nastia Liukin of the U.S., scored only 15.025 in the vault, but soared to victory with the help of a very high score of 16.650 on the parallel bars.

TEAM FINALS

The best eight teams from the preliminary competition take part in the team final. Each team is made up of six gymnasts. The team chooses three gymnasts to take part on each apparatus in the final. All three gymnasts' scores count toward the team total. In 2008, China's men's and women's teams won both team events.

TEAM GIANTS

Traditionally, the Soviet Union and Japan have fought for the Olympic men's team title. Japan won five golds in a row between 1960 and 1976. In recent years, Russia, the Ukraine, the U.S., and China (2008 winners) have also been powerful competitors. In the women's team competition, the strongest teams have come from the Soviet Union (which won eight team gold medals in a row), Romania, China, and the U.S.

Nastia Liukin competes in the balance beam final at the 2008 Olympics. Liukin won a silver in the individual event, but triumphed in the all-around event with a total score of 63.325.

Rhythmic Gymnastics

Rhythmic gymnastics first appeared at the Olympics in 1984. Although performed by men and boys in lower level competitions, it is a women-only sport at the Olympics. Gymnasts require great flexibility, poise, and skill to perform ballet-like routines set to music on a 42.65 foot (13 m) square mat.

Russian rhythmic gymnast Yevgeniya Kanayeva holds an arabesque balance position while keeping her ribbon moving. Kanayeva won her first Olympic gold medal in the all-around competition at the 2008 games.

Superstar

The first ever rhythmic gymnastics Olympic gold medalist was Canadian Lori Fung. She was ranked twenty-third in the world when she entered the Olympics, but scored 57.950 to win the all-around competition.

GETTING TO THE GAMES

Only 24 rhythmic gymnasts take part in the Olympics, so competition in the qualifying events is fierce. The 2007 World Championship was the qualifying event for 2008 Olympics, with the top 20 performers gaining entrance to the Olympics. At most Olympics, the other four competitors are selected to make sure that the country hosting the games, as well as all continents of the world, have at least one gymnast in the competition.

APPARATUS

Five pieces of apparatus are usually used in rhythmic gymnastics: the rope, hoop, clubs, ribbon, and ball. Only four are used in any one Olympic competition. The ball was excluded from the 2008 games, and the 2012 games will not use the rope.

The object is an important part of the routine as the gymnast handles, balances, and moves it around her body. These movements are combined with others, such as leaps and balances, and the whole routine is set to music.

THE RIBBON

The ribbon is 19.7 feet (6 m) long and attached to a 20–24 inch (50–60 cm) long stick. Gymnasts twirl, shake, and spiral it around their bodies, making rhythmic and dramatic shapes in the air in time to the music.

FEATS AND RECORDS
Spain's Almudena Cid Tostado is the only competitor to reach four Olympic rhythmic gymnastics finals in a row—1996, 2000, 2004, and 2008.

A rhythmic gymnast balances the ball on her back while holding an elaborate balance position.

THE BALL

The ball is 7–8 inches (18–20 cm) in diameter and is one of the hardest pieces of apparatus to perform with. This is mainly because the rules insist that gymnasts cannot hold it still in a hand, but must keep it moving or balanced on a part of the body. It can be thrown high in the air, but must be caught gracefully.

Yevgeniya Kanayeva performs a spectacular leap during her hoop routine at the 2008 Olympics. She keeps the hoop spinning around her wrist during the move.

The Chinese rhythmic gymnastic team performs a hoops and clubs routine at the 2008 games. One team member leaps high in a **straddle** position with her legs apart. China won a bronze medal in this event.

THE HOOP AND CLUBS

The hoop is between 2.6–2.95 feet (80 and 90 cm) wide, and the gymnast throws, catches, rolls, and jumps through it. The clubs are each 15.75–19.7 inches (40–50 cm) long, and competitors throw, catch, and spin them, as well as twirl them around in windmill patterns.

THE ROPE

At each end of the rope is a knot. Rhythmic gymnasts skip over it, swing it around, and move it in circles.

FEATS AND RECORDS

Russia has been the most successful rhythmic gymnastics country of the twenty-first century. Russians have won all the Olympic gold medals in both the individual and team competitions since 2000.

INDIVIDUAL COMPETITION

Each of the 24 rhythmic gymnasts at an Olympics takes part in two days of preliminary competitions. At these, the competitors perform two routines each day. The top ten gymnasts enter the final, where they start fresh, performing routines with all four pieces of apparatus to determine who wins the medals.

motion, and a gymnast loses points if she drops it or it rolls away.

SCORING

Rhythmic gymnastic routines were once scored out of ten. This was changed in 2003, and gymnasts are now given a mark out of 30. The score reflects the technical difficulty of the routine and how well it works with the music. Judges look for difficult moves performed with grace as well as moves that flow naturally from one to another. The apparatus must stay in

TEAM COMPETITIONS

A team or group competition was first held at the Olympics in 1996 and won by Spain. Twelve teams take part, with five gymnasts per team performing two different group routines, each lasting up to 2½ minutes. First, each gymnast uses the same piece of apparatus, then two gymnasts perform with one piece of apparatus, while the other three use a different one.

Three members of the Bulgarian team leap high during their three hoops and two clubs routine. The Bulgarian team finished in fifth place at the 2008 Olympics.

Trampolining

Gymnasts first competed on the trampoline at the Olympics in 2000. Individual gymnasts compete in separate men's and women's competitions. They perform routines on a large trampoline that can send them soaring 30–33 feet (9–10 m) into the air. They perform an array of incredible twisting and somersaulting moves in mid-air.

Lu Chunlong of China competes in the men's trampoline final at the 2008 Olympics. Chunlong won the gold medal, Jason Burnett of Canada silver, and Dong Dong, also of China, bronze.

BOUNCY BEGINNINGS

George Nissen, a U.S. gymnast and inventor, pioneered trampolines. He developed the first practical models in the 1930s and gave the sport its name, which comes from the Spanish word *trampolin*, meaning diving board. Nissan sponsored the first trampolining world championships in 1964 and was delighted when it was included in the Olympics in 2000.

FREE AND COMPULSORY

At the Olympics, competitors perform two routines—a compulsory one with set moves, and a free routine in which they

Canadian Rosannagh MacLennan (in the red outfit) and Russian Irina Karavaeva perform their routines on trampolines side by side during the 2008 games.

add their own moves. The eight best gymnasts then enter the final, where they perform a second free routine. All routines start and end with the gymnast standing.

MAKING MOVES

A gymnast starts a routine by building height with a series of bounces while keeping an upright body shape. As their height increases, gymnasts start to perform acrobatic moves. These include the Barani, a forward somersault with a half-twist, and the Adolph, a somersault with 3½ twists. All moves are performed with speed and perfect timing so the gymnast is in the right position when making contact with the **bed** of the trampoline. The gymnast then bounces up again to perform another move. During each routine, **spotters** stand beside the trampoline to ensure the gymnasts' safety.

FEATS AND RECORDS

Karen Cockburn from Canada began trampolining at the age of 11. She won a bronze medal in 2000 and silver medals in 2004 and 2008. She is the only gymnast to win a trampolining medal at three Olympics.

JUDGING AND SCORING

Seven judges score a trampoline competition. Two judge the degree of difficulty of the routine —the more complicated the skills shown, the higher the mark. The other five judges decide how well the trampolinist performs their routine. Judges take points away for mistakes, poor body position, and not completing a move.

Gold Medal Greats

Gymnastics is an intensely competitive sport, and competitors set a very high standard. It is a great achievement to reach the Olympics preliminary competitions, but some gymnasts go further and win medals. Here are profiles of four great Olympic gymnasts.

NADIA COMANECI

Comaneci was just 14 years old when she competed at the 1976 Olympics in the Canadian city of Montreal. She gained a place in history after her perfect routine on the uneven (asymmetric) bars. The judges gave the young Romanian the first ever perfect 10 score at an Olympics. Comaneci continued on and was awarded a further six perfect 10s when she won the individual all-around competition, the beam, and the uneven bars. She also scooped a silver medal in the team event, and a bronze in the floor event.

Superstar

Nadia Comaneci added to her medal collection at the 1980 Olympics, where she won two more golds and two silvers. She later married the gold medal-winning U.S. male gymnast, Bart Conner.

Nadia Comaneci coaches a young gymnast on the balance beam in 2010. She is the only person to receive the Olympic Order twice. This is the highest award for people who have helped the Olympics.

year, she astonished crowds by winning six gold medals at the rhythmic gymnastics World Championship in Mie, Japan—a record that had never before been achieved.

VITALY SCHERBO

Vitaly Scherbo is considered one of the finest male gymnasts of all time. He took up gymnastics at the age of seven, but was not thought likely to win medals at the 1992 Barcelona Olympics. He proved his doubters wrong with a sensational display, winning six gold medals in the vault, parallel bars, rings, pommel horse, the team event, and all-around event. Scherbo also won 12 World Championship and nine European Championship gold medals.

Vitaly Scherbo holds an inverted cross position during the final of the 1996 Olympics. Scherbo won four bronze medals at the games.

LI NING

China's first outstanding international gymnast, Li Ning dazzled audiences at the 1984 Los Angeles Olympics, winning gold in the floor exercise, the rings, and the pommel horse. To these, he added a silver in the vault and team competitions and a bronze in the all-around event. Li won 106 medals during his career, and in 2000 was the first Chinese gymnast to enter the International Gymnastics Hall of Fame. At the 2008 Olympics, he lit the Olympic flame in the stadium cauldron during the opening ceremony.

YEVGENIYA KANAYEVA

At the age of 18, Yevgeniya Kanayeva of Russia was the youngest of all the finalists in the Olympic rhythmic gymnastics competition at the 2008 Olympics. It did not phase her at all as she won convincingly, scoring the highest in all four apparatus routines. The following

Glossary

apparatus   one of the various pieces of equipment, such as the parallel bars or rings, used in gymnastics competitions

artistic gymnastics   a form of gymnastics in which competitors perform routines on large pieces of apparatus

back flip   to leap backward from the ground or balance beam and perform a backward somersault

bed   the area of a trampoline that a trampolinist bounces on

chalk box   a box or dish containing powdered chalk that gymnasts dip their hands into to give them a better grip on their apparatus

coordination   the ability of a gymnast to organize their brain, muscles, and body parts to work together well; top gymnasts need high levels of coordination

dismount   to leave an apparatus at the end of a routine

elite   top performers in a sport

execution   the performance of a routine and how well all the different movements are performed and flow into one another

FIG   short for the Fédération Internationale de Gymnastique or the International Federation of Gymnastics, the body that runs world gymnastics

flexibility   the range of motion through which a body part can move without feeling pain

penalize   to give a gymnast a lower overall mark because of a mistake or poor performance of a skill

release   leaving a bar to perform a move before holding onto it again

rhythmic gymnastics   a competition for women in which gymnasts perform routines on the floor with different objects including a hoop, ball, or ribbon

salto   a flip or somersault in which the feet come up over the head and the body turns around the waist

sequence   two or more positions or skills performed together, creating a different skill or activity

spotters   people who stand on each side of a trampoline ready to help or catch a trampolinist if they should fall or veer to the edge

straddle   a body position in which the body faces forward and the legs are spread far apart to the side

tuck   a position in which the knees and hips are bent and drawn into the chest, and the body is bent at the waist

Books

Gymnastics by Yanitzia Canetti (Cambridge BrickHouse, 2010)

Gymnastics Events by Jason Page (Crabtree Pub. Co, 2008)

Gymnastics Events: Floor, Vault, Bars, and Beam by Jen Jones (Capstone Press, 2007)

How to Improve at Gymnastics by Heather Brown (Crabtree Pub. Co., 2009)

Olympic Gymnastics by Adam B. Hofstetter (Rosen Pub. Group, 2007)

The Olympics: Records by Moira Butterfield (Sea-to-Sea Publications, 2012)

Web Sites

www.fig-gymnastics.com
The official web site of the Fédération Internationale de Gymnastique, the organization that runs world gymnastics.

www.gymnasticsnet.com/amn/usa.html
Learn about gymnastics in the United States, as well as other countries.

www.intlgymnast.com/
The web site of International Gymnast Magazine includes news, features, and interviews with leading gymnasts.

www.usa-gymnastics.org/
The official web site of the organization that governs gymnastics in the United States.

www.brentwoodtc.org/trampolining.htm
An informative web site on trampolining with descriptions and diagrams.

Index